OUT OF THE VALLEY OF DARKNESS

Mary-Etta Hinkle

Out Of The Valley Of Darkness Mary-Etta Hinkle
ISBN # 0-89228-022-0

Copyright © 1992 by IMPACT BOOKS, INC.
137 W. Jefferson, Kirkwood, Mo. 63122

Printed in the United States of America

COVER PAINTING: David Jonathan Hinkle

Cover Layout: S P B Studios

DEDICATION

To Judy, my Jonathan friend, and

To Phyllis, my loyal prayer partner and friend, and

To all the BELOVED, WHOM THE LORD HATH GIVEN,

this book is gratefully dedicated.

The Shepherd's call to His shepherd

When the little lamb falls, pick it up.
When the sheep baas, give it drink.
When the goat rams its horn, give lamb comfort.
In so doing, you will give unto ME.

When the little lamb bleeds, bind its wound.
When the sheep runs away, search its hiding place.
When the goat tears and rends, bind its power.
In so doing, you will give unto ME.

When the little lamb is tired, give it rest.
When the sheep is dismayed, give it hope.
When the goat is belligerent, take authority.
In so doing, you will give unto ME.

When the little lambs skip, enjoy their play.
When the sheep are excited, share their joy.
When the goats breathe death, give back life.
In so doing, you will give unto ME!

Dedicated to **Frank and Ida Mae Hammond**

for their fullfillment of this calling.

CONTENTS

Chapter One
SCHIZOPHRENIA??...............21

Chapter Two
HOW COULD IT HAPPEN?...............25

Chapter Three
ROOTS EXPOSED...............29

Chapter Four
LEAVING THE FARM 44

Chapter Five
LOOK TO THE HILLS
   WHENCE COMETH MY HELP!...57

Chapter Six
YO-YO ON A STRING...............67

Chapter Seven
BILL'S FREEDOM...............81

Chapter Eight
WE WRESTLE NOT AGAINST
   FLESH AND BLOOD...............85

ACKNOWLEDGEMENTS

Dearest husband, Bill, you are my most loyal and supportive stand-by. Even the negatives on your side of the balance scale which you gave me permission to be truthful about, became positive affirmations of God's power to make us overcomers. Indeed you have become a man after God's own heart.

Dear children, Tim, Twila, Bonnie and David, and respective spouses, Audrey, Jerry, and Dana and precious grandchildren, Jessi, Timmy, Jessica, Kristen, Catherine, Jason, Heidi, and Ian, you are a blessing from the Lord. Yes, He "raises the poor and needy from affliction and makes their families like a flock." (Psalm 107:41)

Great appreciation to you, Pastor Dennis, for aiding the Lord in establishing in me self-worth during some difficult years of the testing ground 'desert trek,' following my deliverance out of the "Valley of Darkness."

Thank you, Cara, for your assistance and prayers in the writing of the first draft of this manuscript and, Pam, for the final revision of this book.

And to the many friends and acquaintances over the years that God has used to minister His love and encouragement to me, I extend a heart-felt thankfulness.

FOREWORD

Family life isn't always what it's cut out to be. It takes a lot of doing to become a good family. Everyone has to grow up and it takes time.

I believe everyone should go for counseling early in marriage, to be able to see what they are up against and then be able to ward off the forces which try to hinder a family from surviving.

Take heed, young lovers, and don't wait until thirty years of going through trials and frustrations before realizing that you should have gone for spiritual counsel on how to treat a love mate in marriage.

I praise God for my wife. She has been everything I could possibly want or need in a good woman. She is gifted in many ways - if only I had known how to nurture her talents sooner, I could have saved myself and her a lot of heartaches. You will realize after you read this story what I am talking about. If you have a problem, search it out right away and don't become too proud to ask for help.

I had a dream of a glass cylinder showing our lives being poured through it, and on the inside were thorn-like protrusions which pricked us on our way through life.

Some were sharper and longer on Mary-Etta side of the cylinder than on mine. Later on, in our trip through the cylinder, the thorns were not so frequent or sharp as they were in early married life.

We could have avoided some of these thorns if we had only fully known who our Jesus is, who the enemy is, and how to combat the demonic powers in our lives. Praise God for being so patient with Mary-Etta and me. We are still climbing to the top, but we know we will overcome by always applying the Blood of Jesus to our lives. Amen!

Bill Hinkle
July, 1992

OUT OF THE VALLEY OF DARKNESS

INTO HIS MARVELOUS LIGHT,

OUT OF THE VALLEY OF GLOOM,

OUT OF THE VALLEY OF NIGHT

INTO THE DAWN OF HIS SMILE,

INTO THE CHEER OF HIS WORD,

INTO THE GRACE OF HIS LOVE,

I WAS BROUGHT BY THE HAND OF THE

LORD

PREFACE COMMENT

In our book, *Pigs In The Parlor*, there is a chapter entitled "The Schizophrenia Revelation." This revelation discloses a system of evil spirits which causes the personality disorder known as schizophrenia. There we tell how this "word of knowledge" was initially given by the Holy Spirit to bring deliverance to our friend "Sarah" (not her real name).

Over the years many people have inquired about "Sarah." They have asked, "How is she doing?" "Was she really delivered from schizophrenia?" "Has she kept her deliverance?"

Now, twenty years later, "Sarah" (Mary-Etta Hinkle) gives you her testimony. She tells about her climb "Out Of The Valley Of Darkness." Tears of joy and thanksgiving flooded our eyes as we read the manuscript. "Oh, thank you, Lord, for your goodness and grace. Thank you, Lord, for what you've done for 'Sarah.' Oh, God, may Mary-Etta's testimony bring hope and direction for deliverance to many others who are yet in their own valleys of darkness." Amen!

Frank and Ida Mae Hammond

OUR DESTINY

If there is a mountain someone will climb it.

If a sea, someone will fathom it.

We will delve within the earth to uncover its mysteries.

No problem will be too great to be deciphered.

No atom too small to be dissected.

Even the far-flung worlds we will grasp.

Ours is a vision of life for all who dare to live.

We will forever make conquest.

Written in 1943 for Sis on her graduation as valedictorian of Nickerson High, Nickerson, Kansas by

Edward Harlan Alber

PREFACE

I have been climbing a mountain; one whose path led to the heights of joy. At each turn, peaks of delight lay ahead as majestic fulfillments of God's many promises bestowed over the years I've walked with Him.

Emotional pain accompanied me throughout those years, and even from my earliest recollection, sorrow and anguish of heart dominated much of my life, creating a personal habitat that I'll be referring to throughout this book as "The Valley of Darkness." God, faithful in all things and incapable of failing me, reached out and led me from the Valley.

At its darkest point, this valley was black with gray shadows discoloring even what I would have considered my brighter moments. "I'll engulf you," the shadows threatened. "I'll obliterate even your hope for light; yes, I'll win you for myself," was its haunting message.

My arduous trek out of the Valley of Darkness was accomplished with the victorious love and power of Jesus Christ, Author and Finisher of the faith He gave me, Who for the joy set before Him endured His cross, did not despise the shame, and is seated at the right hand of the Father. My contribution to the process was a willingness to engage in soul searching, deep communion with the Lord in honest prayer, and obedience to His Word as I saw it in Scripture. I came daily (and often moment by moment) into His presence asking, "Lord, what is the answer? What is the way out of this darkness?"

God, I learned over time, does not hastily lead us out of situations, be they sunless, joyless and even sinister, without our own prayerful perseverance and cooperation with His guidance. "Resist the Devil and he will flee..." (James 4:7) are words that inspired my journey. I found, in searching for definitions of "resist": striver against; prevent; defeat; refrain from or abstain from action, and keeping one's self back.

My hope and prayer in writing this book is that the experiences set forth on the following pages will alert others to the shrewdness and craft designs that the spirits of darkness skillfully wield on their unprotected victims, and to show how the personal love and power of Jesus Christ set free those who call upon His Name.

It is not my intent to attribute more than is discernibly valid to the work of satanic powers, for I have witnessed the sad results in lives of Christians who preferred to lay blame on the devil rather than take responsibility for their own misdeeds. Discernment and a willingness to come humbly before God for truth is necessary in making proper diagnosis.

Jesus, my Savior,
died on that tree,
that I might be free.

As I drink of His Spirit,
I will see the person
He wills me to be.

As freedom in His Spirit floats gently down to me,
I'll be fitted to see His plan for my life
and those I meet this day.

He loves me as His child and wants me to be free.
He loves me as His child and wants me to be free!
If I'll only believe in Him, He will set me free!!

as a bird soars,
as the wind howls,
as the sea roars,
FREE!!!

by Twila Majkowski, nee Hinkle
(used by permission)

I will dance to the King.
Will you lift your voice and let it ring?
Will you shout, "Allelulia," to our risen King?
(Repeat)

Our Father, who art in heaven,
Hallowed is thy Name.
May thy kingdom come and thy will be done.

Look around at all the faces,
Many people from many places,
Jesus said to love one another,
Will you honor Christ in your brother?

When I sit and I ponder,
How much the Father does love us.
To think He sent His Son,
To die on Calvary's cross for us.
I've been so many places,
And I've seen so many faces
But the one face I cherish in my heart
Is Jesus Christ in all His loveliness.
I think about His grace,
And I think about His forgiveness,
And as I think about Him, I pray
We may be united as His witnesses.

Written 1979, set to folk style music by Twila Majkowski, nee Hinkle (used by permission)

Chapter One

SCHIZOPHRENIA??

I was finally being delivered of that dark spirit, jealousy. Frank and Ida Hammond were praying for my deliverance, one of our many sessions toward my complete freedom. As Frank spoke to the spirit within me, I realized jealousy had become an odd pal, tagging along through life's situations, cleverly disguised as something quite unrelated to its true nature.

While they commanded its release on my life, voices dominated my mind. 'You know these people don't really love you.' These words, surfacing over and over again during the ministry, had effaced much of my self-esteem, and had affected every area of my home, extended family and church friends. Jealousy's disguise made it difficult for me to accept its existence, but when the fog cleared and release came, the Holy Spirit filled that void with the assurance of God's love and that of His servants' also.

I suddenly realized I could never satisfy the god of jealousy. When I gave it gifts, it demanded more. If I bought its favor, it repaid me with abuse. When I appeased it, it retaliated with anger. The more people helped me in the natural, the more wounded they were, and the more lonely I became. God's deliverance was my only source of freedom. The writer of Song of Solomon writes,

"Set me as a seal upon thine heart, as a seal upon thine arm: for love is strong as death; jealousy is cruel as the grave; the coals thereof are coals of fire, which hath a most vehement flame."

I had felt far more than the godly jealousy, the carefulness to be righteous, to be "jealous for God's laws." I had even been accused of being jealous of my own children. Seven years after my deliverance, my closest friend, Judy, declared, "Jean, I have never seen a jealous bone in your body in the three years I have known you." She could not know how that testimony thrilled my soul.

But losing the spirit of jealousy was just one step in a process that took several years and incorporated several kinds of deliverances. Although Frank and Ida Hammond ministered to me over a seven year period which included receiving the Baptism of the Holy Spirit, various forms of counseling and deliverance, providing the majority of my freedom through their prayers, they were not the only ones who ministered to me. Once I lost a spirit by not "giving it place" in my life. The Holy Spirit orchestrated my deliverance and used many vessels for ministry as He saw fit.

When the Hammonds were frustrated and saw no lasting results from their prayer sessions with me, God revealed to Ida a pattern of spirits and how to pray against them. That revelation and deliverance they recorded in their book *Pigs in the Parlor*. Parts of that revelation jolted me, especially the title of schizophrenia. But by the end of my journey, I could say with James in chapter 3:18: "And the harvest of righteousness (conformity to God's will in thought and deed) is (the fruit of the seed) sown in peace by those who work for and make peace (in themselves and in others, that peace which means concord, agreement, and harmony between individuals, with undisturbedness, and in a peaceful mind free from fears and agitating passions and moral conflicts)."

If the untangling of my problems was complex, the building of the problems was more so. Relationships in my childhood home were like so many other families' during the Great Depression, sublimated to earning a living. While we struggled and worked we were unable to recognize the roots of our discord. The mixture of our two, sometimes three, family units was a financial necessity for all involved, but helped to fan the flames of family disunity, and made a nest for the spirits that tormented me through much of my life.

Even the ministry to me was at times a source of conflict. When Ida Hammond disclosed her revelation to me, I was astonished, anguished, that her diagnosis was schizophrenia. I did not understand the revelation and God's interpretation of it initially. After suffering for five years under the stigma of that, Judy, a friend, ministered a healing to me for that specifically. However, the schizophrenic pattern that God showed to the Hammonds was a valid pathway, a picture of a web that had entangled me for years and had me confused, hurt, and lonely.

Because readers frequently ask the Hammond's about "Sarah's" progress, as I was named in *Pigs in the Parlor* for privacy's sake, I intend to let my readers experience my victory, a victory that affected not only me, but my husband and children also.

Why are skies so dark at times one cannot see the light?

Why are days so black at noon it seems that it is night?

Why do disappointments come and tear apart all dreams?

I cannot answer one of these, but I know Jesus leads.

Why is life so complex and it seems trials never end?

Why do sorrows sadden days and God seems slow to tend?

Why do loved ones walk away from His o'ershadowing care?

I cannot answer one of these, but I know He is there.

Chapter Two
HOW COULD IT HAPPEN?

How does Satan make inroads in Christians' lives? We have power over him by using the Name above all others. How then does he deteriorate the lives of believers? Some say a Christian can not possibly have a demon because we are temples of the Holy Spirit; that would be a house divided against itself. The Hammonds encouraged their readers and those to whom they ministered to regard themselves as body, soul (intellect, emotions, will), and spirit. God's life inhabits the spirit of a Christian, which comes alive at the new birth. It is our responsibility to guard our bodies and souls, which can become doorways to spirits that oppose the Spirit of God. Repeated disobedience to God's laws "gives place to the devil."

When Satan entered Judas, it was obvious only to Jesus. Jesus foretold that Peter would yield to the temptation of darkness, that fear that resided without Peter's knowledge. Today we see many of God's people falling, committing acts of unrighteousness after being seduced by the Evil One. The degree to which Satan has access to our lives will depend upon the degree to which we have made Jesus Lord in our lives. The areas we close to the full inspection of Christ are vulnerable to another occupying force.

Some Christians find it difficult to accept that satanic power can be at work in the lives of believers, and some Christians discount the entire doctrine of demons, which frees Satan to build strongholds in even the most far reaching Christian ministries. These same Christians dismiss over two hundred scriptures that name Satan's activities using his various names and warn about the master of deceit and his methods of destruction. He is without honor, infiltrating even the lives of innocent children. Never does he play fairly. Satan's intention is to create fear of himself, since fear is a form of worship; or disbelief, in order to work undetected, and better yet, let God take the blame for his own work. However, just the mention of Jesus' name and pleading the blood of Christ binds his power.

Jesus commanded demons to leave His followers. Sometimes He demanded names from those spirits before commanding them to depart in order to expose their activities. If only one demon driven from the Demoniac in Mark 5:9 entered each pig, Jesus delivered that man of two thousand spirits ruled by a prince called Legion.

Luke wrote in the eighth chapter that seven demons left Mary Magdalene. Jesus recognized the need of people to be delivered from various spirits; at other times He healed, discerning the need in their lives. He drove out demons whose manifestations were both physical and psychological, as is shown in Matthew 4:24 and many other passages.

Satan also enters through unhealed wounds, neglect, unforgiveness, trauma, and especially fears. He built fortresses, strongholds (see 2 Cor. 10:4) of rejection and rebellion in my personality to the point that I accepted thoughts and attitudes in my mind as my own. No one in my family intentionally hurt me, but their actions inadvertently left openings for the devil to do his work. Praise God that He did not leave me tormented, but His Spirit has been at work preserving me and delivering me from my enemies.

I have included poems written to me by family members for my ninth birthday, which show that my family loved and cherished me.[1] There was no human conspiracy to convince me I was unloved or unlovely. But their capacity to feel and demonstrate love was not sufficient to keep me shielded from the evil design Satan intended for my life. Even in the most wholesome families, where love is fully expressed, Satan can convince us we are hated. The word of God and the gifts of the Spirit are our sure defense. They also became my offensive weapons.

---

1. Copies of the poems are on pages 43 and 44.

O, discordant notes,
Notes that exist because of the fall.
Come alive!
Change your key!
Change your tempo!
Enter into league with the Creator.
Give back harmony,
And out of confusion let peace reign.
Give back joy
Abounding into infusion of reality.
For Jesus is real.
He's the One who gives
>   *Vibrancy,*
>   *Meaning,*
>   *LIFE!*

Chapter Three
ROOTS EXPOSED

The Lord spoke to Ida Mae and defined schizophrenia as "a disturbance, distortion, or disintegration of the development of the personality...the fingers on your hands represent the nest of demon spirits that make up schizophrenia." These spirits "came into this person's life when she was very, very young."

In the Lord's instructions He advised Ida Mae that this deliverance was a process that would take time, in order for me to adjust to the discovery that so much of my personality is not the real self. I would need time to adjust, and to fall out of agreement with the false demon personalities, point by point. I would have to come to loathe the schizophrenic personality, which I had used to compensate for the hurts and loneliness, by such activities as fantasizing and self pity. However, the ruling demons of rejection and rebellion were the last to go and the strongest to battle. They were the core of the schizophrenic. The controlling demon, Schizophrenia, called Double Mindedness in the Bible, is described by James in 1:8:

"A double minded man is unstable in all his ways."

The Amplified translation expands it:

"a man of two minds - hesitating, dubious, irresolute - unstable and unreliable and uncertain about everything (he thinks, feels, decides)."

The phrase translated "two minds" comes from a compound Greek word literally meaning "two souls." (*Pigs*, p. 124-5)

A few weeks later, as the Lord showed Ida what demons each finger of the hands represented, He told her the controlling demon, Schizophrenia, invited other demons in to distort the personality. It commonly begins in childhood or infancy, and sometimes while the child is in his mother's womb, but it always begins with rejection. The causes for rejection may differ, an unwanted pregnancy, or an unsettled home, but rejection is the "door."

I was like a yo-yo most of my life, being bounced from rejection to rebellion, and never experiencing the true submission to the Lord. Rejection had the strongest pull upon me. Because of our German ancestry, my family were firm disciplinarians, and rebellion was not able to flourish as well while I was in their care. Rejection, however, grew stronger and stronger in the austere environment of the Kansas plains following the Great Depression.

Seven years before I was born, my family experienced a devastating, tragic fire. As a minister my father met with opposition more than once. After warning one member in his congregation to leave his particular sinful lifestyle, the man angrily planned ways to destroy my father and each member of his family.

My mother detected the fire he started in their two story farmhouse while all were asleep in the upper bedrooms. She tried to alert everyone in time for escape, but highly flammable liquid had been sprayed about the house, so the house went up quickly in fierce flames. My father was the last one out and burned so badly he was not expected to survive. Before escaping, he wrapped up two-year-old Sis in blankets and hurled her still sleeping from a bedroom window. She was unhurt. My brother Ed suffered no life threatening burns, but had deep psychological fears. He slept with a loaded gun by his pillow for many months after the fire.

My brother Clement was severely burned and only lived for two hours. Only the bones remained of my older sister, Miriam, who was overcome with smoke. When Father attempted to rescue her, the floor gave way beneath him, forcing a quick leap to safety and a broken leg in the fall.

Witnesses to the scene of the fire provided enough evidence to imprison the hateful man from Father's congregation. Although authorities offered to put bloodhounds on the trail of the suspect, Father would not prosecute or condemn one of his flock. Vengeance belonged to God, and He would repay. At the root of his decision not to press charges was his love for the flock he tended, and hope that this lost sheep might be saved by forgiveness and mercy, something stronger than iron bars.

While Father was strong in his convictions, we family members suffered intense fear that this murderous man would some day strike again. For many years after the fire, we met him on the sidewalks of town; each time I shivered with dreadful fright. This constant fear made avenues for the powers of darkness to deteriorate my life. I did not realize how much until, at the age of thirty-seven, I was delivered of a spirit of fear. During the deliverance I was transported in my mind to this same childhood fear. The same man was entering my childhood bedroom window to harm me, and I screamed in terror as the spirit left me.

Father was fifty when I was born. Although psychologically healthy, Father was in poor physical condition. Bone tuberculosis had shortened one leg six or seven inches. Special consideration had been given my father by his parents because of his disability; he was the only one of twelve children to go to college. An infectious eruption of the dormant disease prevented Father from obtaining a degree. Later he took college courses by correspondence. He supported us as a farmer and was an ordained pastor of an independent Pentecostal church for twelve years.

Mother was forty when I was born, but looked older after the fire seven years previous and all the anxiety that followed it. Her pregnancy with me was planned to be a compensation for the two children they had lost in the fire. While her body fed me the physical nourishment I needed, I was also the recipient of her grief and depression. The predisposition to schizophrenia is believed to be hereditary. Because she had never been emotionally strong, my mother probably experienced deeper mental anguish than any of us realized after the ordeal of the fire. Years later I realized that Satan's intent was to continue and expand that torment within me.

My first four years were fairly secure. Our family was forced to move into my maternal grandmother's home during the Depression of the Thirties. The five of us, including Sis who was nine years older than I, were comfortable in her little five-room house. Ed, my brother twenty-one years older, was in the military then.

Mary-Etta Jean was my given name, and Mother wanted me called "Mary-Etta," but for several reasons I rebelled against it. I threw a fit if anyone called me Mary-Etta. So the family complied and called me Jean, with the exception of Father's relatives. Mother did not research

32

names when mine was chosen, but I believe God directed her in her choice. Mary means "anointed" and Etta is a derivative of Henrietta taken from Henry, which means "home ruler." Jean means "loving God." Therefore, my name means "the anointed home ruler who loves God." God planned me from my beginning; the names fit today. I answer to either, but prefer Mary-Etta.

I was always secretly elated when Mother compared me with Grandma. Though she was a stern disciplinarian, Grandma was a woman to be admired. I wanted to emulate her strength, especially because Mother was not one I could cling to. The pride she took in a clean, neat house made me feel comfortable and respectable. I remember watching Mother and Grandma make exquisite quilts which they sold for five dollars to contribute to our needs. My life might have been more secure had she lived beyond my early years.

Grandma's death was the first of several, each two years apart. Sis broke the news to me when Grandma died by simply giving me the information and leaving, thinking I was too young at age four to appreciate the situation. She left me in an overwhelming state of sorrow. Grandma, my strength, was gone; to whom could I turn for consolation? I exhibited unusually hyper-activity that demanded attention at her funeral. "Act your age," I was admonished. My emotional needs were not recognized or met.

The root of my emotional problems were not addressed in my school experiences either. At the insistence of my parents and against the advice of my first grade teacher, I began first grade at age five. Had I waited another year, there would have been no other first-graders in our one-room country school of eight grades. But I was one of four first graders entering that year. While other students were reciting, I was often sent outdoors to play, and dismissed from school earlier than the others that school term.

In spite of this, I learned to read that year. My mother's missionary sister, Aunty, came home on furlough and she taught me to read. I was delighted; I loved to read and study and quickly moved into second grade reading materials. Fairy tales were my favorites because they assisted my escape into a make-believe world where everyone lived blissfully ever after.

Fortunately, the school board hired a different teacher the following year. When I became disobedient to her, and the story of my poor conduct was reported to my older brother Ed, he calmly cut a tree branch and spanked me. He took no pleasure in it, and I held no resentment against him. From then on I behaved, and that teacher granted me an early promotion to the third grade.

I desperately needed attention. But my aunt returned to the mission field, and Mother was laden with a heavy work load that included full time nursing care for Father whose health was failing, washing with a scrub board, and heating water on the cook stove. It was no one's intention to overlook me, but for long periods of time I was left alone.

Responsibilities were thrust upon me at an early age. When I was six, my oldest nephew three months old, Ed and Rose's son, was left in my care for an afternoon. Reading my book, I rocked him by curling my toes around the rung of his carriage. Pulling it back and forth, I managed to keep him asleep until Ed and Rose returned from working in a neighbor's field. Later I helped with the care of all of their four boys.

Father's mother died when I was six. I recall her as a kind woman. I only shared a small portion of her affection because she had so many grandchildren from her twelve children. Family pictures taken the day of her funeral reveal Father's poor health. Soon afterwards he was bedfast and remained so for two years, until his death the summer before my eighth birthday.

Ed was in the field plowing when Mother realized Father was dying. She instructed me to put aside the basket of clothing I was ironing and in a voice of panic said, "Jean, run as fast as your legs will take you and get your brother." Again, deep sorrow struck my heart, and once again in all the busyness of preparing for the funeral, I was overlooked. I had whooping cough and therefore was not allowed to attend the funeral.

"Don't get near her," were the words I heard said by relatives to their children, who were deemed more worthy to pay respects to Father's leaving than I. This rejection, during a time when feelings of abandonment were already high, caused me to enter more deeply that world of fantasy where I was insulated from pain.

No one could guess, least of all me, that Satan was building strongholds through the wounds I received. Loneliness, fears, frequent detachment from reality, and rebellion were all open doors for the devil to do his work in me. Hosea warned, "My people are destroyed through lack of knowledge." (4:6) Had my family known what was happening, I am sure they would have worked to mend the breaches in my psyche.

Fear was a frequent tool in Satan's arsenal. I wrestled it my fourth grade year while walking back and forth to school each day. Though the school building was only a field mile across from our home, the most direct route could not be traversed by a child because of the impassible creek and livestock fence. It was a two-mile hike by two alternate routes; the one I chose allowed me to walk with other children along the way. I walked it in snow, sleet, rain and sun until a bully, three years older and far heftier than I, took a disliking to me. He left bruises on my arms and slapped my face. More than once I came home in tears.

On one occasion, however, the attack took place on the school steps. Our family did not use profanity, but I borrowed a word from this bully and shot it back at him. The new teacher observed what happened and blamed me, issuing an embarrassing punishment, but neglected to even reprimand the bully.

Ed decided I should walk to school by the alternate route, which deprived me of companionship. It was a busier road, paved, and very frightening to an eight-year-old. How could it happen, I wondered, that I should be so strictly punished for another's cruelty? This incident further convinced me that the best defense against hurt and loneliness was withdrawal. As I walked those two lonely miles each day, I tried to convince myself that walking alone was enjoyable, adventurous, bold. Daydreaming made time pass more quickly. Withdrawal became a friend that later, during deliverance, I came to recognize as an enemy and renounce. In the meantime, it became a foundation in the schizophrenic pattern to build webs of insecurity, timidity, unworthiness, condemnation.

When I was eleven, I was sent to work on a neighboring farm for the summer. We still did not have adequate finances, therefore, it was necessary for me to contribute to the family finances. I lived with the family for the summer, only visiting home a few weekends. I was paid one dollar each day, after eight hours of hard work, including housework, sheep herding, and babysitting an incorrigible nine-year-old boy.

The next summer I worked for two families and did these same chores in addition to cooking when the mother and her two girls were not at home. Dinner meals were served to both the family and hired hands. All leftovers had to be thrown away according to the mother's instructions. I was horrified to see the waste of roast, chicken, and other perfectly good foods. Even their dogs could not consume it all. I thought them very wealthy. Why were they so favored when I had so little?

I had progressed so well in school that at barely thirteen years of age I began high school. My body was growing also; I wore a size ten shoe. The preceding summer, instead of all my wages going to Mother, who spent it on my necessities, my employer decided to put some of my earnings aside and purchase a pair of sturdy shoes for me. Thank the Lord my feet stopped growing! It was not easy to buy attractive and functional shoes in that size, so I suffered teenage humiliation every time someone gazed in the direction of my incredibly ugly shoes. I never owned more than one pair of shoes in a given year. Today I am apt to go barefoot around the house, but in my closet there are numerous pairs of pretty, high-heeled dress shoes.

I can recall numerous happy childhood memories, such as cavorting in the snow drifts, and the snow tunnel Ed took time to carve for me. There were many happy hours of play with my favorite cousin, Johnny, who though retarded, was never able to advance beyond the maturity of a twelve year old, but could play the piano beautifully by ear. I especially enjoyed sleeping with Mother in her feather bed. She beat the mattress vigorously with a broom handle to make it high and airy. I climbed onto a chair and leaped into the fluffy down to snuggle up close to Mother and sink into sleep.

However, even in the happy times I never felt "safe." I never was confident that "Mommie and Daddy are taking care of me." I was expected to always behave in a mature and responsible manner. I resented Mother because she was not a capable, emotionally stable person, able to command respect and discipline. Discipline was adminis-

37

tered to me by numerous "bosses," and contention often arose between the "bosses" and Mother about how I should be treated.

Though I respected my father, he was sometimes harsh in his discipline and failed to openly demonstrate affection and tenderness for me. I honored Father, but resented his untimely death. Even in middle age, I remember being left out of the family group circled around Father's bed when he died. My heart sorrowed as an adult because Father did not tell me good-bye.

Father had never taken me on his knee or given me an affectionate hug, so learning intimacy with my Heavenly Father became an awkward challenge. When a friend, Donna, encouraged me to crawl up and sit in the lap of my Father God, I instantly saw in my mind's eye a little girl sitting most uncomfortably, trying hard to resist the impulse to jump down and run.

Because I had not bonded properly with my earthly father, I found bonding with my Heavenly Father difficult also. Only very recently, John Duncan, a pastor associated with Frank Hammond, advised me to allow God to pursue the bonding issue by resting the matter solely with Him.

God provided a large measure of healing regarding my father's death when I attended a retreat directed by a prominent Christian theologian and psychiatrist. The focus of the talk was the emotional distress caused by the death of people we love. After the retreat I had a dream relating to Father's death. When I awoke, in a vision I saw Father standing beside God the Father. Tears blurred my sight as I cried in anguish, "Daddy, Daddy, why did you leave me?" God's word ministered comfort to me. He made me know "I will never leave you, nor forsake you" (Heb. 13:5), and "when thy father and mother forsake thee, then I, the Lord, will take thee up" (Ps. 27:10).

This ministry and that of a friend's, Mary, brought a peace to my soul. Mary prayed with me and helped me thank the Lord for Father's death, which brought release. God was at work to heal the hurts and untangle the web. Layer by layer God brought healing.

If Father's death left me feeling abandoned, Mother's presence made me feel more so. Constantly I felt the pressure to perform in ways that would assure Mother I loved her. I was painfully aware of Mother's fragile emotions. There were many times I needed a mother to talk with, but unwilling to contribute toward Mother's further mental stress, I held my thoughts and feelings inside.

I looked to Aunty to be a mother to me, but I felt she would never accept me in the same manner she accepted Sis. She was also accustomed to the strict, compliant obedience of mission children. I did not fit the mold.

Years before when Ed left the military, he and his wife Rose joined us on the farm, after Grandma's death. They assisted Mother tremendously with the management of it. Mother and Aunty inherited the farm from Grandma when she died; it was our only means of income during those Great Depression Years and the financial depression of our family in the years following. There was no government aid to women with dependent children.

Ed had given Father a deathbed promise he would always look after Mother, a promise he fulfilled for the remainder of her life. Though Mother became an excellent financial manager and left a small inheritance to us children, she did not even know how to write a check when Father died. Consequently, she leaned heavily on Ed for support and advice. Mother and Ed formed a partnership which excluded Rose from the business transactions, but not the heavy work load.

39

Rose had come from worse deprivation than we had experienced, and excluding myself, it was generally agreed that she ought to have been more grateful for the privilege of being part of our family. Rose was considered beneath Ed in intellect and breeding. We were from good German and Swiss heritages and Mennonite background. Ed had a college education and had researched the family name to important people in history, including Mattheus Alber, a reformer and friend of Martin Luther. Though we were poor as church mice and had problems common to much of society, we suffered many feelings of inferiority, and pride in our related aristocracies showed itself in our attitudes. Naturally, Rose felt the sting of those attitudes and reacted with jealousy.

I loved Rose dearly and loved tagging after her. She loved being the mother of their four boys, who lit up my life. From the day they arrived home from the hospital in two-year intervals Rose and I shared the mutual joy and care of her boys. They entertained all of us at mealtimes and brought laughter into our home with their cute talk and comical ways. When Ed and Rose took occasional outings, they left the boys with Mother and me. Mother disliked the responsibility, which I gladly accepted. A loving bond exists between us today.

Ed once remarked, "Do you know why poor people have so many children? It's because they can't have anything else. "As it happened, the children were responsible for keeping Ed and Rose together until the youngest was eighteen, when they divorced. Two of their sons became ministers; one has a doctorate in Divinity.

Mother was becoming less and less emotionally stable. From time to time she suffered nervous breakdowns and mental eccentricities. Unable to cope with the challenges of life, Mother locked herself in her room for days, wailing and crying. On occasion she reached out to me for comfort. I reacted with great discomfort and quickly departed, spending as much time as possible in the farmyard. One time I was so distraught I fled the house running as fast as my nine-year old legs could carry me. How could I, struggling with my own lack of identity, fulfill my mother's need?

In addition to Mother's mental condition, Aunty arrived home a second time during my eight-year stay on the farm. This time she was a different person. She had been sent home from the mission field because of a physical problem during surgery. Accompanying emotional side-effects caused her to form a quick attachment to Sis, who was able to provide care and understanding.

I was once again, quite ignored. I wondered what I had done wrong. How could I have become recognizably unlovable since Aunty's previous visit? Three years before I had basked in her affection, drinking it in like a thirsty plant; now I was thrust off. No one took the time to explain the situation to me, not even when I asked why Aunty didn't love me any more. Inner voices transmitted the messages "You are not loved, you are not lovable."

I clung to Rose whose actions reflected love to me. Our common rejected status, whether real or imagined, formed a bond between us. Jealousy forged it tighter. Mother wrote a poem with a message of love for me, but I was unable to receive her love properly, because of the great emotional upheavals she manifested. I now know the demons within me prevented my receiving her love also.

As an adult I realize that Mother felt the most unloved of any of my family. I am aware that early in my life our roles were reversed. Burdened with the need to prove my love for my mother, I endeavored to gain her approval. As a child and as an adult, I was criticized by members of my family when I attempted to talk out the frustrations I felt over home situations. Consequently, I locked the distress I felt in a guarded closet in my mind. How could a child be expected to understand what adults were not able to decipher either?

When the relationship between Mother and Rose deteriorated, Ed sent Mother East for a visit to relatives. She returned much improved in mind. Mother and Rose attempted better relations, but had invisible crusts to dissolve before friendship could be developed. Though their fellowship was not severed, the relationship never became open and cleansed. The relationship between Mother and Rose called for separation when I was about thirteen. Ed bought Mother a small house with a loan from their friendly banker, and for a few more years he and Rose remained on the farm. That event marked a time of upheaval and loneliness for me, until I was able to live with Mother again when I was in high school.

Nickerson, Kansas
Sept 6, 1943
Labor Day

My Dear Mary-Etta Jean:

The friendly things you do and say,
Your smiles that brighten every day,
Have made me realize anew,
Life's finest gift is a daughter like you!

May future with her kindest smile
Wreath laurels from your brow,
May loving angels guard and keep thee,
Ever pure as thou art now.

As ever,
Mother

To My Sis:

Some clock ticks every little moment
    slipping silently away.
It will tick while you are sleeping
    or by time of day.
You can waste each precious moment
    while at work or school,
But remember you are wasting - each -
    a precious little jewel!

Yours while the sands of time
come running down a generation,

Edward Harlan Alber

---

1. These notes have been set in type, since the original handwritten copies would not
have reproduced well.

Sept 5, 1943

Dear Jean,

When twilight pulls the curtain,
And pins it with a star,
Remember that you have a nurse,
No matter where you are.

Your Big Sis,
Gloria

I have only just a minute,
Only sixty seconds in it,
Forced upon me,
Can't refuse it,
But it's up to me to use it.
I must suffer if I lose it,
Give account if I abuse it,
Just a tiny little minute,
But eternity is in it.

Rose

Nickerson, Kansas
Sept 6, 1943

Dearest Jean -

"Keep a watch on your words my darling,
For words are wonderful things.
They are sweet like newly made honey,
And like bees, have terrible stings."

"When the cabin burns down and all
   is spent,
Come live in my heart and pay no rent."

Lots of Love,
Aunty Erma

Chapter Four

LEAVING THE FARM

When the relationship between Rose and Mother began to break down, Mother was the one to leave. Her first attempt at employment proved quite temporary, but another job opened ten miles away in Hutchinson, Kansas, as a maid in the hospital were my sister worked as head nurse in the polio ward. Sis had completed cadet nurse's training during World War II and worked herself into a responsible position. Unable to drive, Mother could not commute to work from the small home Ed had purchased for us. Mother rented a sleeping room for herself after arranging accommodations for me with Sis and her first husband, Arnol.

I enjoyed living with Sis; Arnol was a loving big brother to me, but was killed in an automobile accident seven years later. While living with Sis, I worked after school at a local cafe bussing tables and washing dishes. The work I did not mind, but I despised serving fellow school mates. These were the same teens whose friendship I wanted when I tried to mingle with them at our local drugstore. I always felt I was on the outside looking in.

After two months of this living arrangement, Sis and Arnol moved away to care for his dying father. Shortly before they moved, Sis and Arnol invited me to an exciting night in the city with them. I gave up my job to go; this was the first time I ever had fun.

After they left I lived alone for two months, eating very little, feeling afraid, rejected, and abandoned. The guilt that I could no longer contribute to Mother's meager income kept me from taking advantage of Mother's grocery charge account she had instructed me to use. As a result, improper diet and emotional stress contributed to my feelings of lethargy, and finally illness. Years later the illness was diagnosed as probable rheumatic fever.

During the Christmas holidays while visiting with Ed and Rose, I was very ill. Sis and Mother met to confer about my living arrangements. No one seemed able to take me in. I leaped from the divan where I was privy to their discussion, stamped my feet across the room, and shouted in angry tones, "It's too bad I'm such a bother to everyone! Someone is going to have to take care of me, because I can't stand to stay alone any longer!" Venting my frustration and rebellion did not bring soothing results. I still felt rejected and full of self pity.

Mother saw that I visited a doctor and a month's dosage of sulfa was prescribed. Mother then hired a school teacher to board with me, an arrangement that lasted three months and drained more than half of Mother's income. This teacher eased my feelings of abandonment by frequently inviting me on weekend visits to her parents' home.

Mother was not uncaring. She told me how worry for my welfare nearly made her sick, but prayer and faith in God's providence comforted her. Though widows and orphans are commanded in God's word to be cared for by the church, I do not recall any assistance from our local churches.

After Father died we were seldom able to attend

46

church for various reasons. Mother insisted we listen to Charles E. Fuller's "Old Fashioned Revival Hour" and "The Lutheran Hour." The "Old Fashioned Revival Hour" was my favorite because of the pianist, Rudy Atwood. When I began to play the piano, I endeavored to emulate his performance of "Heavenly Sunshine."

The Rural Bible Crusade opened a memorization program in our little country school when I was ten. Mother spent almost every evening reading scripture passages to me. I learned five hundred Bible verses, many of which I still remember. I can recall always having a hunger in my heart for God, and believing the good news that Christ died for our sins and rose on the third day as Savior and Lord.

Also instilled in me was love and acceptance of God's people in all denominations. Mother told me how preju-diced toward other denominations she and Father had been before the fire. But people of every denomination minis-tered gifts and love to them, which changed their perspec-tives. Her most repeated phrase was "At that point (after the fire), Daddy and I got off the judgment seat and onto the mercy seat, and I don't ever intend to change my view." In spite of Mother's emotional weaknesses, she gave me a powerful heritage of faith through her gospel messages. Later, that tenaciousness for God's love helped me gain my freedom.

Aunty's arrival home from the mission field for the final time marked a time of considerable peace for me. This ended my living arrangement with the school teacher. Aunty immediately redecorated the house, making it pretty and cozy. After the shabby appearance of our farm house, this new decor was wonderful to me, especially as I began to acquire a few "upper crust" friends and lose some of the inferior feelings I had. Aunty was asked to speak at some of the church clubs in town and related her missionary experiences. After eating Aunty's delicious cooking I quickly gained twenty attractive pounds. A handsome, red-haired, young man (not my future husband) began to pursue me, and I attended school events with him.

Seven months later, Aunty and Mother sold some farm land to purchase a house in Hutchinson. I entered a school that had excellent academic ratings and received a superlative music education. Aunty, a good entertainer, served meals in five courses, so I learned social amenities. My only complaint was the volumes of dishes after those banquets. So my high school years were normal and free of unusual stresses.

I met my husband-to-be when I was fourteen; he was twenty-three. Driving a 1948 Frazer, in attractive apparel, and endowed with beautiful, red, wavy hair, Bill was very appealing. His slight stature did not bother me. I was proud of him. After a period of adjustment to the news that I intended to marry him, Mother and Aunty voiced their approval.

Bill, believing I was at least eighteen, began pursuing me energetically. He had not dated for about three years after being painfully spurned when he was in the armed forces. Now past the hurt, he was praying that God would provide him a wife.

When Bill discovered I was only fourteen, he decided to discontinue our relationship. I did not intentionally withhold my age from him; the subject just never became an issue. Had he actually lost interest in me, I would have released Bill, but our age difference was not reason enough in my eyes to sever our relationship. With unabashed tears I begged and pleaded with him to stay. When I was fifteen, just eleven months after meeting Bill, he placed a diamond engagement ring on my finger, and seven months later we were married. At Mother's insistence I finished high school, and then entered business college at Bill's urging.

Our wedding day was memorable. Two hundred guests graced the church ceremony; one hundred of them came to the catered reception, completely arranged by Aunty. Money I had saved, along with help from Mother and Aunty, provided precious wedding memories that carried me through many challenging years to follow. Thirty years later our oldest daughter walked down the aisle on her father's arm in my own wedding dress. Although there is little evidence today that a beautiful church wedding contributes to a solid marriage, ours certainly did. Our wedding was the first time I realized that I was cherished, and my heart opened wide. We spent our honeymoon in the beauty and peacefulness of the Colorado mountains.

Bad news brought me harshly back to reality. I was informed that Bill's mother was not in favor of our marriage. She considered me too "worldly" to be part of their very legalistic Christian family. The Biblical Christ, to them, was a dictator pronouncing do's and don'ts. Half the family followed Jesus by maintaining the letter of the law; the other half lived in rebellious indifference.

Bill's mother's words ruled. If his mother said I was worldly and thus unacceptable, Bill and his seven siblings concurred. It hurt me deeply that I was relegated to the position of an outsider and made to feel like my presence was an imposition on them. I tried to align myself by various methods to fit both sides, but attempts in either direction only brought greater frustration to me. Bill did not realize the responsibility of his marriage vows to "...leave father and mother and cleave" to his wife, becoming one flesh. (Matt. 19:5; Eph. 5:31). Because Bill needed his family's approval, unable to suffer any rejection from them, he was unable to defend me when necessary. In addition, he was insensitive to their coldness toward me.

49

At the same time he was experiencing the royal treatment from my family. He gave them the impression he was a loyal and attentive husband. It was thirty-three years before Bill could step completely out of the control his family exerted over us.

I realize now, from study, prayer, and observation, that children who experience emotional stress to the degree that I had, often build defense mechanisms to protect their wounds. I had a number of those characteristics that were not easy to embrace or understand. What wounded me the most was that the people who rejected me in Bill's family were also professing Christians. I did not understand their lack of kindness, nor their judgmental criticisms. Years later I realize that each believer is an unfinished work. At that time I was not secure enough to deal with their criticism, instead, I was continually being confirmed as rejected.

Within our own home, Bill and I enjoyed some of married life's pleasures. He was an attentive father, a good provider financially, and we were sexually compatible. However, relationships between me and his family did not improve.

Bill and I both entered marriage with certain expectations, requirements, and fears concerning each other. Because Bill's mother was a licensed minister of the Gospel, he had been raised in a Christian home, and his behavior was moral, I assumed Bill would be the spiritual head of our family. When I found he had no intention of even attending church with me, I felt I had been deceived. Bill expected me to stay home, tend the children and his own needs, and settle into mediocrity.

I felt I was cast into a role that paralleled the critical view Bill had of his mother who he thought was overly involved in church activities. The more determined I became to serve the Lord, the more affection, time and money he withheld from me and spent elsewhere. This was part of the pattern of Bill's rebellion against religion. He cannot be blamed for disliking the particular legalistic form of Christianity he had known, but for too long Bill was determined to protest any and all church affiliation.

We had been married long enough to have three children, when one day I received an alarming phone call from someone in Bill's family. I was verbally assaulted with filthy words, and told his family did not love me, which hammered at my emotions for years. Family members held me responsible for the attack. Years later I learned that a lie told about me precipitated the attack.

The demons within me were quick to hammer, 'You are not loved; you are not lovable.' I lay awake all night listening to those dark spirits dictating their venomous lies designed to destroy me. By morning I was convinced: I was not lovable. I was not even worthwhile, and I deserved to be hated.

Standing in front of the bathroom sink, razor in hand, I tried to muster enough courage to end my worthlessness. The phone rang. Like a robot, mechanically I answered and heard the voice of my neighbor, Mary-Ruth, who felt impressed to phone me that morning at 8:30. As a night person, she rarely rose earlier than noon.

Hearing my incoherent voice, she hurried over and exclaimed, "You are crazy to blame yourself after all the junk I've seen you endure."

Her attempts to console and strengthen me cut through to my senses, and shook me from the depression that had gripped so forcefully. Just having someone remind me of my worth at that point lifted me from the abyss. Before courage left again, I picked up the receiver and phoned one of Bill's relatives.

"If ever that episode is repeated," I declared, "I will take Bill's children and exit all your lives, and even Bill will not see us again!"

This was a bluff, because I could not support three children alone; but it worked. Before the day was over, I learned that Bill's mother had come to my defense finally, and with immeasurable gratitude I relaxed and allowed peace to resettle my soul. From that day forth, my mother-in-law and I shared as good a relationship as I believe is possible between mother and daughter-in-law.

I now know that God was at work to save me from my enemies and bring me out of the valley of darkness. Shortly before the assault, I dedicated my life to Jesus. Although Bill nor I realized the timeliness of that act, retrospection made me appreciate God's direction. I had known Him prior to that time, but had not released my life to His care. As a result, He rescued me then, and continued to touch us both with restoration, although we experienced many battles in the meantime.

Satan always schemes to destroy fellowship between people who have been happy. He comes like a lion from the woods to rend and tear, and his attacks are swift, surprising, and powerful. Although today I am free from the excessive response to the assaults of people and demons, I do not appreciate deliberate disregard of my dignity. The phrase in a Christian chorus is "we'll save each man's dignity." The night I was so viciously attacked, my dignity was shredded like raw strips of meat.

It was not God's will for our home to be broken as I had threatened, but I felt I had no recourse. Satan works to great advantage where a spouse is abused, but God had releases planned I had not envisioned. Not long after this

52

battle, Bill and I moved our family to the Rocky Mountains. While working in Denver, we were able to view their grandeur every day. With less interference, we began to enjoy one another more in an atmosphere of freedom. Little did we know we would also enjoy greater relationships with Him.

Mothers are usually happiest,
    when their children are all around.
But they're apt not to know from one minute to next,
    what their younguns will have planned.
It might be an ocean excursion,
    a visit to foreign lands,
    a journey far to the planet Mars,
    or a trip to the house of a friend.

Children keep her busy all through the day,
    thinking up things to do,
And they never know from moment to yon,
    how to even tie their shoes.
They are probably slopping around unlaced,
    with the strings dragging the mud,
    jacket unzipped,
    cap awry,
    and gloves in the house in the tub.

Children are such a happy bunch.
    (if adults could be the same!)
They seldom worry about anything,
    or whether they have a good name.
They just sail by from day to day,
    enjoying life as it comes,
    with little concern 'bout tomorrow,
    because they have a home.

Children have faith their mothers and fathers,
    will take care of all of their needs.
If we could only walk with our Heavenly Father,
    and be as assured as He leads.
Parents will forgive their kids,
    when they act naughty and wrong,
And they don't expect these little ones,
    to be all grown up and strong.

Mommies and Daddies love little tykes,
*   just the way they are,*
*   even when they're filthy,*
*   and have raided the cookie jar.*
If we could be as certain,
*   our Father loved us that way,*
We'd be a whole lot happier,
*   as we run and play.*

After all, don't we know,
*   we are children at heart?*
Why don't we relax a bit,
*   as our lives we daily start?*
Wouldn't we be more contented,
*   if we'd give folks a break,*
*   reaching out hands to greet them,*
*   and giving a friendly shake?*
Children rarely meet a stranger,
*   and seldom know one exists.*
They have to be taught to fear people,
*   and there are mean one who persist,*
*   in robbing of the pleasure,*
*   God intended a child to have.*
Let's extend Jesus' blessing to children,
*   and to them, His precious love give!*

MARRIED 39 YEARS

WEDDING BELLS

FATHER
(Note his built-up shoe)

SIS, ME, FATHER, ED, MOTHER

AUNTY AND ME

COUSIN JOHNNY AND ME

TWILA IN MY WEDDING DRESS

TWILA, BONNIE, TIM

DAVID

Chapter Five

LOOK TO THE HILLS
WHENCE COMETH MY HELP!

For years my mind was influenced, not only by memories of loneliness, but by crippling voices that took advantage of that loneliness and tried to persuade me to commit suicide. I did not have the slightest notion of the source of those voices; I was experiencing satanic attack and did not recognize the enemy or how to defeat him.

In our new mountain environment, in a supportive congregation, I was not as vulnerable to those voices. Bill and I were active in our church, and our fellowship with Christ was also growing. Scripture came alive to me; it seemed to leap from the pages with understanding and a sense of Christ's presence in addition. I was learning so much that I was asked to instruct the Sunday Bible class.

While one side of me grew by leaps and bounds, there was another part of me I hoped would not be revealed. Bill knew the other side existed, but he did not understand it and was unwittingly used by Satan to trigger it. I shared with Christian friends how I had come out of the emotional abyss after committing my life to Jesus, but did not allow them to see the troubled area of my life that even I could not explain. With grit and determination, I acted like a

Christian and was so successful that ladies called me for counsel thinking I had all the answers. I was so unable to continue the front at home that Bill believed there were two of me, but did not know how to deal with it. At the same time, friends complimented us with "I can sure tell you two are in love," and "you and Bill go together like two peas in a pod."

I became an important person around town, which bolstered my hidden, damaged ego. I was voted "Outstanding Young Woman of America," and my name was placed in a who's who book. I had the honor of playing "Clair De Lune" on the piano at a Republican rally, and then accompanying my best friend who sang a solo for the guest of honor, the governor's wife. A pastor's wife told me she had considered nominating me for Mrs. America because she thought I was the most efficient, perfectly all-together woman she had ever known. It also came to my ears that a Christian neighbor referred a friend needing advice about rearing children to me, because I was such a competent and gifted mother. Whew! What a far cry from the sobbing, crumbled wreck I was the morning I wanted to end it all in a stupored daze!

The praise of people offered temporary relief from my problems, but did not heal them. The weak spots remained without the touch of the Master, and eventually they became grounds for attack again. I needed discernment and God's power to be released from the satanic bondage that flourished during our early marriage and the arrival of our four children. Although those years were precious with many lovely memories, even then, Satan was perverting my perceptions and reactions to situations. Jealousy especially was a strong enemy driving a wedge between me and Bill and our first son, Tim.

Tim arrived when Bill and I had been married two years. I yearned to be a mother and had fervently prayed that God would give me a child. I loved being pregnant and even enjoyed the birth, because Sis remembered her promise; she was my private nurse through most of the labor and all of the delivery.

After five days, I took my new baby to Mother and Aunty's home until I could travel the sixty miles to my own home when Tim was ten days old. It was a household of women: Sis and her three children were living there while her husband was overseas. Aunty revealed a wonderful secret. After all the years she had given up marriage and children to serve the Lord, she decided to wed. Sis and I were ecstatic, but Mother became excessively distraught. Auntie had been an anchor to her. Because of Mother's behavior, depression and stress descended upon me, and my milk supply dried up.

As Tim grew, the knowledge in me grew that the delightful baby boy I expected to bring me ultimate joy was replacing me in Bill's affections. I began to feel left out. The psychology books caution young mothers not to leave the new fathers out, but instead, once again, I was on the outside. Bill had been taught that boys belonged to their fathers and girls to their mothers.

When Tim was just one, I leaned down to Bill while he rested on the divan and gave him a hug and kiss. Noticing this, Tim came toddling across the room protesting. I was quickly waved away by Bill.

"Go on and leave me alone. Quit making Tim jealous!"

Needless to say, I began to think Bill had prayed for a wife only to have a son, and any old wife would suffice.

Tim was well-behaved when Daddy was not around, but changed quickly to a demanding, fit-throwing terror around Bill. When I tried to do anything with Tim, he screamed, "I want my daddy." I gave up any attempts to control the situation. Sis admonished me during a visit, to take charge or rear an incorrigible brat.

I was not without experience. I had extensively helped Rose and Ed with their four boys; and later in my teens, I assisted Sis with her three boys. I felt I had acquired a respectable amount of expertise in the field of discipline. Non-injurious spankings were part of that discipline, but Bill's response was frequently bizarre. He sometimes took the small stick from my hand and whacked me with it, laughing while Tim watched. Interference rather than support began to undermine my discipline of Tim and later with our two daughters. As a result, I applied nearly all the discipline, because to warn the children to wait until their father was home was ineffectual. Daddy posed no threat to anyone except me.

This split in discipline only reinforced my feelings that Bill did not defend me. From the beginning of our marriage I had yearned for Bill to protect me from the criticisms of his family. However, our first crisis concerning discipline did not occur until Tim was two years old. We had moved to Denver, Colorado when he was eighteen months old, and our relatives had come for a visit.

Driving home from a family picnic, relatives informed Bill and me that they disliked visiting with us because of Tim's disturbingly naughty behavior. I felt I was being unjustly accused, again, because I was being blamed for behavior I had tried to correct and had argued with Bill about for two years.

Absorbed in self pity, I refused to get out of the car when we arrived home. Their remarks, unexpected and cruel, were more so because of my severe sensitivity and vulnerability to rejection. So serious was the harsh threat of their opinion, that it was fourteen years before meaning-ful, enjoyable fellowship was restored between us.

I sat in my fragile emotional condition, slipped past sullenness into a full-blown suicidal depression. Drown-ing in the nearby river was as vivid as a movie screen in my mind. Satan quickly took advantage of the situation.

Once established, suicidal thoughts recurred through-out the following years as a ready solution to any desperate circumstance. That demon of destruction had a room full of movies and grabbed the most suitable one for me whenever my mind welcomed them. As each death scene rolled, the additional condemnation whispered, "You don't have the guts or the courage to take your own life."

The following morning, a Christian young mother, Muriel, knocked on our door. She was greeted by some-one who looked strangely familiar but was a blend of me and a prize-fighter. My eyes were puffed almost shut, but Muriel saw past that to my sorrowing heart. Her caring friendship at that moment offered understanding that gave me courage. The Lord was always faithful to send helpers, and I welcomed them all. After this painful incident, Bill eased his interference.

Our second child, Twila, arrived when Tim was two. I would have preferred another boy because I feared the unfamiliarity of rearing a girl. The obstetrician who as-sisted me determined I should not gain more than sixteen pounds during the pregnancy and twice prescribed diet pills containing amphetamines. He did not realize the danger of drugs to my unborn child.

Twila arrived a nervous baby, crying a great deal with frequent stomach upsets. She became the busiest little person I had ever seen, even climbing fences before she was a year old. If I glanced away from her, she was gone in a flash. Acquaintances remarked how nervous I was trying to keep up with her.

I felt hostility toward Twila because she was so like myself. Between her second and fourth birthdays I reacted to her antics with intolerance, even sticking her in a closet for punishment. She appeared to be unbothered by it, playing with this and that interesting object while cloistered. I never used that form of punishment on the other children, but it was so effective with her, though cruel and unwise.

Later, in her early twenties, a prayer team ministered to Twila. While in prayer a member of the team saw a vision of a small child in a closet. Twila had lost the memory of the experience, and later asked me about it. I immediately asked her forgiveness for it. By this time I realized I had provided ground for fear and rejection to enter a little child, and I was deeply sorry for punishing her that way.

Tim was not jealous of his sister; he enjoyed the role of big brother. Bill loved taking the children to the circus, amusement parks, and outdoor activities. Our backyard was grand central station to all the neighbor children, which I welcomed in a contrast to my lonely childhood.

Bonnie was born when Twila was four. But before her birth we moved from a small mobile home into eighteen hundred square feet of living space. I expected this one-story, brick house with a basement to be a source of comfort and joy after the mobile home, but we found ourselves surrounded by hateful, gossipy neighbors whose mission was to control everyone around them.

This was not a paranoid reaction on my part. The distress these particular neighbors brought to another neighbor caused her to demand her husband sell their house and move away. Though Bill was not happy about the neighborhood, he was not as troubled because he was working during the day. Caring neighbors across the street criticized Bill for not defending me. To this day, Bill and I have a dislike of suburbia.

Tim developed his first of three bouts with rheumatic fever, while I was pregnant with Bonnie. For six weeks he was not allowed to walk and had to be carried. That was difficult, but not as threatening as contracting mumps.

Corline, the wife of Bill's employer, nursed me through the mumps. Even she could not prevent premature labor in the seventh month, so I was hospitalized. My Christian sister-in-law, Lenore, requested a twenty-four-hour prayer chain in her church on our behalf. In answer, I carried Bonnie to term. When I gazed on that new little redhead, I was filled with gratitude and an overwhelming love for her. I quickly realized I had not felt that for Twila. I repented, and determined to be more loving toward her.

There was someone else who desperately needed love, myself. Frustrated over neighbors, relatives and illnesses, my feelings of being unloved mushroomed into an enveloping cloud. Even the caring efforts of friends did not remedy my feelings of depression. I begged Bill to take me to a psychiatrist. The cost of counseling would have been prohibitive, but I interpreted his refusal as proof that I was not loved.

I attempted to find solutions in books dealing with emotional problems, and finally, against Bill's instructions not to, I called our preacher. His counsel was "the Lord has been giving you a good spanking." He advised I join a ladies' Bible study class.

The Bible study became another step closer to freedom for me. While there I rededicated my life to the Lord, and some of the torment subsided. One of the ladies in the group told me that depression was a tool of the devil. I needed to rebuke the depression in Jesus' Name and plead the blood of Jesus over it.

The very next morning I awoke enveloped in that familiar shroud. Immediately a small voice instructed me to do as Doris had said.

Another voice countered, "Isn't that the stupidist thing you've ever heard?" I wondered what could be hurt if this "taking authority" did not work. I'll never forget what happened next.

Some force started at the bottom of my feet and began to roll up like a curtain shade until I actually felt something move up my body and lift right off the top of my head. Immediately everything looked brighter.

All I had said was "Depression, in the Name of Jesus you have to go, and I plead the blood of Jesus over you." That was just the beginning of God's plan to set me free. I needed more deliverance, but that particular church taught nothing about deliverance. I know that by drawing near to God, He drew near to me and brought a piece of the truth that would one day set me totally free. Eight years later the Lord moved us into fellowship with Christians who did know about deliverance.

A PROPHECY

"Come, ye tattered and torn.

Listen to the voice of your Saviour.

He is calling, 'Come and follow Me,

For I have the answer to your problem.

I will not despise.

I will not despair.

All power is displayed in Me.

I have known all things from the beginning of time.

I formed you.

I created you.

Not one thing is hidden from My view.

Look up and live.

In Me is life and health and strength to meet every emergency and come out victorious over evil.

Look unto Me, ye ends of the earth.

You suffer unduly because you have not realized

that in Me lies the answer to your every need.

I love you. I love you. I love you.

In Me you have life, health, peace

> *abundantly now and forevermore."*

Chapter Six

YO-YO ON A STRING

When Bonnie was three, Bill had an opportunity to work in the mountains. He and fellow carpenters camped at Hoosier Pass above Breckenridge to begin building the first cabin on the Blue River when skiing became a boom in Summit County. Presently there are many beautiful homes and condominiums all the way to the summit. Bill's grandfather, father and five brothers were all carpenters; Bill was a carpenter until we went into a family business.

Rather than stay home in Denver, we wives packed what we needed and joined the men at the work site. It was a herculean work effort to hike down a hill for water, cook meals on a camp fire, scrub clothes by hand and hang them on trees to dry. The men caught fish in the river each evening after work, so we had numerous fish fries of delicious Rocky Mountain trout.

The children played outdoors, getting filthy as rot, making rafts on which to float down the river, and watching beavers build their dams. Each Saturday evening we scrubbed them up to attend church and Sunday school the next morning.

When Bill's work continued through the winter months into December, we rented a hundred-year old log house and moved even the piano Bill had bought us from Denver. I patched a hole in an outside wall large enough to stuff a cat through, bought paint, and cleaned that charming house. We considered ourselves adventurous pioneers.

The first week in our log house, while eating supper, Twila exclaimed, "Daddy, a little birdie just flew through the kitchen!" Bill tracked the 'birdie' and discovered it was a bat that had entered through a broken attic window. Once that was covered and the bat disposed, we had no more bats in our belfry, at least not literal ones.

Tim and Twila attended a little country school across from our house. They were so close we enjoyed lunch together, away from the city pressures, amid the beautiful mountain solitude.

When Bill's employment ended and he was forced to return to Denver for work, I determined to stay in the mountains with the children, to spend my days baking, sewing and mothering. The first winter we had unprecedented fifty below zero weather, so cold we were forced to wrap ourselves in coats and blankets as we sat around our one heating stove. When we all came down sick at once, Tim went to the home of a newly married Christian couple, Darrell and Kathy, for help.

They brought the only doctor in that area who practiced on weekends at the ski hill. He put us back on the road to recovery with some medicine and a shot for Twila. Because of Darrell's witness, Bill began attending church with us when he came on weekends. We had several months of happiness in the mountain hide-a-way.

On crisp winter evenings we donned ice skates and walked a block to the pond for some wholesome fun. The children inherited Bill's athletic ability, and cut figure eights around me, but I gave it my best shot. All the adventure of skating and mountain climbing was shortened when we were forced to move back to Denver the following winter.

Living in Denver returned us to the negative influences that activated Bill's rebellion toward me. Shortly thereafter, I had to be hospitalized for two weeks in neck traction for a ruptured disc in the cervical spine. With a warning from the doctors that surgery might be necessary, I was fitted with a neck brace and sent home. I was in constant pain for a year. Sparked by my nagging about helping me with the housework, Bill struck me so severely I feared he had broken my already injured neck. This act of violence and his general lack of concern for me caused a deep well of anger, even rage against him in me.

Bill ventured into a family business which failed and brought greater stress into our lives. I felt more anger and rebellion against him when he gave his family several large financial gifts.

There were times when I considered retaliating against Bill's unkindness by withholding sex from him as punishment. But, ironically, sex was the one area of our lives that was relatively free, and I knew that misusing our one, deep and honest expression of unity would most surely end in divorce.

We spent six months back in Denver together. I came before the Lord weeping and bargaining. "I am willing, Lord, to live like a pauper if you'll only give me a Christian husband and home." In a few short weeks we returned to the mountains.

Six months after leaving the mountains, we returned to Frisco where the Lord enabled us to buy a small, fairly new, mountain cabin. Christian friends who sold us the cabin allowed us to take over the existing loan at a very low rate and no down payment. We were dead broke and bought a second house. The Lord effected a miracle!

It was located on a high hill; from the road below we climbed thirty-eight cement steps and a flight of stairs to the front door. We did not have to add exercise to our routine. The cabin originally had two levels with 768 square feet of living space, but during the course of the next twelve years, Bill added on. When we sold it, the cabin had 2200 square feet with an attached carport. God began to bless us with some of our happiest days then, and I believe it was because we began to tithe.

Bill bought the family a Husky snowmobile, a very small caterpillar tractor that pulled an attached sled with enough seating room for everyone to pile on and ride at the top speed of 29 miles per hour. Frequently, as late as nine in the evening, Bill invited us all to go up the mountain. With our cheers of excitement, we bundled up in several layers of clothing, including face masks.

> As we climbed the packed hiking and snow-
> mobile trail,
>   We'd oft break the path on new recent snow,
>   And hear little night animals scurrying out of
> our way,
>   Making fresh tracks in the fallen snow.

Bonnie prayed for a dog and several days later Bill's brother, Rex, came to their work site with a little stray.

"Bill, your kids need a dog."

When Bill arrived home that evening with that dirty, mangy creature, Bonnie squealed in delight.

"I didn't think God would answer my prayer, but He did! He did!"

Sandy, transformed by a bath and grooming, slept on the foot of Bonnie's bed, and lived to be fourteen and a half years old.

Our piano became another important aspect of our lives. I had begun to play by ear at a very early age. My mother recognized my talent and arranged music lessons in the ninth grade, as did the school's choir-band teacher who said I had the talent to become a concert pianist, but lack of money prevented the extensive music study I desired.

In Frisco I became the organist and choir director, and often sang solos for church. I taught my youngsters music until they each entered high school. Twila was able to pick out tunes by ear, and Tim played his first piano piece for a first grade performance.

When Bonnie was five, we formed a mother-daughter trio. The girls carried their own harmony against other voices. Bonnie sang soprano, Twila high tenor soprano, and I sang alto. We were invited to sing in several churches. Occasionally Tim joined us for a quartet and Bill accompanied on his harmonica. God was dear to us; I dreamed we would be an evangelistic singing family.

We lived determined to display to the world how a Christian family is supposed to act. We were successful outwardly, and our home had the appearance of a well-ordered existence. We did not have a television, but entertained each other with family and church life.

Bill had begun to smoke at the age of thirty-five, but smoking was discouraged in our congregation. He hid the addiction from the church brethren, and since he had been elected a deacon in the church, I, feeling guilty, protected him in the deception. I worried about his health because of his wartime lung injury. But after joining the Fellowship, he was delivered of a spirit of nicotine and has not smoked since.

When Bonnie contracted three-day measles, I caught them from her. I was pregnant a fourth time and did not respond to gamma globulin administered by our physician. Six weeks later, in the fourth month, a threatened miscarriage began. After being hospitalized, it was determined the fetus had been dead four to six weeks. In surgery, a curettage was performed, after which a severe cervical erosion erupted and refused to heal. A hysterectomy was recommended, which I refused. I was not sure we had all the children we wanted yet, so physically I dealt with the problem for the next year. In retrospect, I am very glad I refused.

Word was filtering through the Christian community that Pastor Frank Hammond had "gone into some weird stuff." With my background in Pentecostalism, I recognized the "weird stuff" as the move of the Holy Spirit, and I wanted to follow along.

The Hammonds invited me to attend a Kathryn Kuhlman meeting with them in Denver. What a glorious night that proved to be! I witnessed miraculous healings all around me. Relatives of those healed were weeping and praising God as His power swept through the assembly, just as in New Testament times.

The little servant of God, Kathryn, assured the audience there was nothing special about her, but that the power came from the Holy Spirit. She exhorted us not to grieve Him. She called out a healing from the podium, and at that precise moment the power of God touched my head, coursed through my body and centered in my female organs. I felt a glowing, warm, pulsating light bulb had been turned on inside my body. A voice spoke to me saying, "I have healed you."

Believing those words, I kept a doctor's appointment I had previously made. He gave me a clean bill of health, confirming what I believed.

The same night I was healed the Hammonds ministered the baptism of the Holy Spirit to me. After the initial experience, I did not immediately pray in tongues, but three words came in pictures across the screen in my mind, and I spoke them. They sounded like Spanish or some other beautiful Romance language I had never learned.

I returned home ablaze with the fire of the Spirit, and eagerly devoured the Word of God in a way I had never before enjoyed. At noon each day, after spending time in the Bible and prayer, I raced around to catch up on the housework. About two weeks later, while praising God, the floodgate of God's Spirit opened and I prayed in tongues. The Lord also gave me songs with which to praise him.

It was no wonder that when Bonnie was ten, after this marvelous healing, I became pregnant again. I had wanted four children and felt Satan had cheated me from having one more. During the healthy pregnancy the Lord told me I should name the child David Jonathan, meaning "the beloved the Lord hath given." Bill was not convinced I'd received a word from the Lord and was picking out girls' names the day of his birth. I knew he would be a boy.

David was an anointed child. From the age of three the Lord moved in him in unusual ways. Tucking him in one evening, I noticed his angelic smile.

The Lord said to me, "I'm showing him a picture of myself."

I asked David, "Did you just see Jesus?"

He smiled a contented smile, "Yes, Mommie."

He was like having a little prophet Samuel around; he frequently came to me, "Mommie, this just came into my head..." and then told me about a picture he saw portraying a Biblical scene. I dropped everything to sit with David and tell him about the Bible story he had seen in his mind.

When David was five, a family moved across the street from us with two children David's age. He had so few play-mates, I was glad to see these children befriend him. One day while David was playing in the yard of their apartment complex, the Spirit spoke to me urgently, "Mother, go across the street and get your son; a homosexual spirit is after him." I flew out the door, down the hill, crossed the street and arrived just as the door of the game room was being locked by the children's sixteen year old half-brother.

"David," I called, "it is time for you to come home and nap now." The door was unlocked. While David napped, I prayed and felt impressed to visit the mother of those children, taking along a Christian book. She began to pour out her heart to me, telling me what a terrible trial the older son was, that he had even been servicing homosexuals on Denver streets. My heart sorrowed for this mother, but rejoiced at the confirmation of what God had spoken to me and His protection of David.

I never asked David to pray for me; I never wanted to put any pressure on him to perform. But numerous times throughout his childhood, in times of trial that followed, he came to me with wonderful counsel from the descriptions of the pictures in his head.

His pictures contained discernment, wisdom, and

exhortation. Once he sketched a detailed picture of the positions Bill and I held in our argument-in-progress.

With the gentlest tones he said, "Mommie, you must quit hitting Daddy over the head with that rolling pin (not a literal one). You think you are waking him up, but you are only knocking him out." Money and time in a counselor's chair would not have accomplished the change in my behavior so readily. The advice became prophetic; Bill was soon "to wake up."

David became an artist and woodworker. He was a very normal boy and as a teenager tried a few flings. But I rested in confident assurance that he belonged to Christ. When he left home to join the Air Force, I was left with a wrenching loss and again warred with the spirit of depression to maintain my equilibrium.

The letter he sent home helped:

> I loved my childhood, Mom and Dad, and I owe all to you and our Christian home. I've thought about it a lot, how everything I can come back to is good and not bad. A lot of the people I know didn't have the past life I've had. They never talk about home or wanting to go back there, because there's nothing for them to go back to."

Reading that letter, I sat and cried. I wished I had been as good a mother to the other three children as I had been to David. I wished their memories of home and parents contained his positive words. At the same time, I praised God for His healing which had resulted in this son, for His deliverance, and His grace. He had promised to "restore the years the canker worm has eaten" from Joel 2:25-27.

I wish I could testify that receiving the baptism of the Holy Spirit and my beautiful healing brought all the joy and happiness we sought. Both experiences were steps to freedom from the valley of darkness I walked. The baptism especially stirred up the demons I had had since childhood. The following years were filled with turmoil, but the demons could no longer stay hidden, and the Lord began to reveal their presence to me when I was strong enough to confront them and there were people who knew how to minister to me.

The year preceding my receiving the Baptism was a year of unhappiness and stress. I lost a dear friend because she was involved in an adulterous affair which necessitated church discipline. My mother also came to spend the summer with us, which magnified all my unresolved childhood torments. At that time I did not know demons had anything to do with the daily mental bombardment to which I was being subjected.

After receiving the baptism, I experienced a season of joy. The Lord poured out a spirit of praise on me, and I spent much time singing the songs He gave me and praising Him.

But instead of the dark, carefully guarded, area of my life receding, it began to intensify and become less controllable. I found I was unable to play the actress successfully. Some friends even suspected I was playing a role. Feelings of rejection were magnified, because many former Christian friends did not approve of the baptism in the Holy Spirit. Honors formerly bestowed ceased. But I was invited to minister with the Hammonds, and God honored my requests for healing and deliverance for others, although I had not been delivered myself as yet.

The more ministry I was involved in, the more Bill buffeted me at home, and the more rebellious I became.

Rebellion and rejection had me on a yo-yo, bouncing me back and forth between them. I was not a godly woman in my conduct toward my husband.

Members of the fellowship only saw my rebellion. Bill appeared a passive personality, and no one could believe he was capable of abusive behavior. No one believed me when I tried to tell them some of the previous hurts I had endured, so even in the fellowship I was strengthened in rejection. I became more rebellious.

I had no idea that I was soon to be delivered of those same enemies. The Lord gave me a scripture in the meantime:

> "For thy Maker is thine husband; the Lord of hosts is his name; and thy Redeemer the Holy One of Israel: the God of the whole earth shall he be called. For the Lord hath called thee as a woman forsaken and grieved in spirit, and a wife of youth, when thou wast refused (rejected), saith thy God.
>
> Isaiah 54:5,6

I realized that Bill could never be the all-in-all that I expected. Only the Lord could fill that place.

Marriage is a wonderful institution,
Ordained by God in His infinite love.
He knew the bone He took from Adam,
Could be fitted for Eve like a glove.

It takes a lot of time and planning,
And each have to yield a bit.
Both need to walk with the Savior,
If everything is going to properly fit.

Love, married love, is a wonderful gift,
Only a wise Father could bestow.
May each couple who name the name of Christ,
Let that love singly and jointly show.

On eagle's wings,
We'll fly away,
My love and I
While it's yet day,
So we can see the world beneath,
While we climb high above the reef,
And we'll soar high above the strife,
Of earth's vain hopes and its demise,
For we are free to live and love,
For God our Father reigns above.

God the Father sent His Son.
Death's final chapter to be won.
And He imparts His life to us.
Whate'er life holds,
His will is just.

My love and I,
We've known much pain,
But in living life there is great gain,
For life is good if one knows how
To give and cherish a fragrant flow'r.
The flower starts but from a seed,
Yet grows to be a beauty freed!
So 'tis with life when one lets go,
And lives God's fullness of love to show.

God the Father sent His Son.
Death's final chapter to be won.
And when He rose to victory,
Resurrection power made us free!!!

Chapter Seven

BILL'S FREEDOM

Sixteen years before we moved to the Rocky Mountains, my husband Bill lay in a foxhole, a shrapnel wound just half an inch from his spine. A buddy had pulled him into the hole and covered him with an overcoat. The next morning he was transferred to a field hospital under heavy shelling. The World War II truck hit a shell hole and threw Bill out of the truck. He suffered temporary memory loss, paralysis of one side of his body, and a collapsed lung. He was sure he would not survive. He vowed, in his prayer, he would serve the Lord if he did.

Bill had postponed keeping that vow. Although his wartime wounds had healed, he was spiritually crippled by his passive rebellion against his family's harsh religion. Bill saw God as a harsh dictator, not someone with whom he could have a loving relationship.

After moving to Frisco, high in the majestic mountains, their breathtaking beauty shining through the windows of the little church, Bill committed his life to Christ, who was even then replacing his concept with fresh, tender revelations. Joy bells also rang in my heart; now both of us were committed to Him.

Bill's commitment allowed God to break him free of the religious bondage he had endured. Second Corinthians states "the letter of the law killeth, but the Spirit maketh alive." (2 Cor. 3:6) Demons seeking inroads into Christ's church manifest themselves in more cunningly deceptive ways than in secular environs. Scripture describes their movements as "in sheep's clothing." Some of the highest ranking demons are religious spirits, for example, those demons that develop sectarian deceptions.

Jesus said to those bound in religion, "Woe to you, teachers of the law and Pharisees, you hypocrites! You shut the kingdom of heaven in men's faces. You yourselves do not enter, nor will you let those enter who are trying to enter." (Matt. 23;13,14, NIV) Too many Christians only see the obvious sins of adultery, murder, and drunkenness, but do not discern the religious ways Satan captivates believers.

If we are to win the war against our enemy, Satan, we must know who our enemy is and how he operates. Some say all a Christian needs to know is our Commanding Officer. Did America defeat Germany in World War II because all the men on the front knew who General Patton or General Eisenhower was? As Christians we need to know more than that also. When Jesus said we will do greater works than His, our assignment was to win lost souls, heal the sick, and cast out demons. Casting out demons was emphasized on the Apostles' first missionary detail. But most Christians would not know a demon if it came up and bit the end of their noses. I didn't. God had won our souls, but healing and deliverance were not even imagined to us then.

God began to deal with Bill in another area of failure, the area of discipline. The story of Eli in the Old Testament tells of the consequences of failing to discipline children. Eli, a leader of God's people, refused to walk in

82

obedience and as a result God judged him and his sons. Their disobedience was a stumbling block to the Israelites who came to worship.

> "For I have told him I will judge his house forever for the iniquity he knoweth; because his sons made themselves vile and he restrained them not."
>
> I Sam. 3:13 KJV

Fortunately, Bill was obedient after he committed himself to the Lord and began to hear God's admonitions. Bill began to break up Satan's strongholds in his life by renouncing all rebellion toward God's commands, and all spirits passed from generation to generation, especially those that resulted in poor discipline. Bill asked my forgiveness for his failures. I released him from my unforgiveness.

I now consistently will to forgive. My emotions don't always feel like I have forgiven, but my feelings fall into line with my decisions eventually.

God's timing was wisdom. I needed Bill's understanding and prayers in the struggles for my freedom in the years to come.

The love of Jesus is the strongest love on earth.
He shed His Blood because He loved me so.
His love surrounds the boundless reach that is my heart.
It's a love that will not ever let me go.

The love of Jesus comforts me in every trial.
He is my strength in every step I take.
He leads me ever upward and I bask in the smile,
Of the love He gives me every morn I wake.

The love of Jesus through me heals the wounds and
scars,
Of those who have been battered by the foe.
It gives them peace and comfort as they journey on,
For the life of Christ within me wills it so.

Oh, the anguish of the Savior!
See Him hanging on that tree.
He who bore our every sorrow,
Will He not grant joy to thee?

Give Him all your hurts and yearnings.
Let Him make pure your life within.
He will open heaven's portals,
And give you grace in pain, to win.

He arose; proclaim the glad tidings.
He arose; He arose from that grave.
He arose; proclaim the message.
He arose; and He's mighty to save.

Chapter Eight

WE WRESTLE NOT AGAINST
FLESH AND BLOOD

"How long must I wrestle with my thoughts and every day have sorrow in my heart? How long will my enemy triumph over me?" Psalm 13:2

Very often I have heard believers advise not to pray for something unless you are prepared to receive it. How very well this applied to me when, after some weeks of tormenting relationships with Bill and our teenagers, I began to pour through the pages of scripture for help. I stomped my feet across the living room floor and shouted, "I have tried and tried to live this Christian life, and I am sick and tired of trying! God, if you can do anything with me, You are welcome to try!"

I had been studying Romans for several weeks, deliberating on the bondage of the law versus the wonderful grace of Jesus. I realized I was as guilty as the foolish Galatians, who thought they could be made perfect by the flesh.

I knew my flesh was not going to hold out. "Lord," I cried, "show me the key; show me the key." Every facet of life was distressful to me at this point, and I was wearing out my Bible in study.

Before I was baptized in the Holy Spirit, I was susceptible to infections and frequently ill. Several weeks after
experiencing this renewal, I suffered a bout of illness and
requested Frank and Ida Mae pray for my healing. As we
prayed words came to my mind, 'You are frequently sick
because you want to be. As a child you received affection
when you were ill.' I repented immediately of this foolish
desire to be sick. Sickness had not brought me any attention during my marriage. Bill did not treat me with tender
affection when I was ill. I praise the Lord he didn't, or I
might not have been as eager to lose this dependence.

Frank bound the spirit of infirmity and cast it out of
me. This spirit is named in Luke 13:11,

> "And there was a woman there who for eighteen
> years had had an infirmity caused by a spirit (a
> demon of sickness)."

Deliverance from that spirit was effective; I was not
sick once the following a year. For twenty-five years I had
had a strep throat infection once a year. One time hospital-
ization was required for recovery. I was susceptible to this
infection because of the bitterness and resentment I chroni-
cally felt. I know I have been set free of that spirit of infirmity, because I have had no strep infections since that
day.

Though causes vary with individuals, certain diseases
are rooted in spiritual rather than physical causes, as is seen
in the ministry of Jesus. Sometimes He simply healed the
people, at other times He called out a demon that caused
the person to be sick.

The doctor had advised a woman I knew to have her
gall bladder removed. After receiving deliverance from a

spirit of bitterness, the symptoms disappeared and surgery was not necessary.

Research claims stress is a strong factor in a large number of diseases. Scripture teaches in Proverbs 17:22 that unhappiness affects the bones.

> "A cheerful heart is good medicine, but a crushed spirit dries up the bones."

Deliverance ministers have found there is a strong correlation between resentment and arthritis. I recently read a testimony of a woman who, because she had an abortion, opened the door for the enemy to afflict her with lupus. When she confessed the abortion as murder and was delivered of that spirit, the Lord healed her of lupus.

My freedom from the root of bitterness was effected in stages over a period of years. Every time I thought the Lord had completed the work, He allowed some other trial to tickle that spirit. As I dug deeper into my soulish self and threw away more trash from dank and moldy closets, the bright sunlight of Jesus penetrated the corners and the root of bitterness shriveled in the intensity of His love.

The Holy Spirit revealed that I was under a curse of death. The curse was traced to the murderous intent of the man who set fire to my parents' house. If Satan's ultimate intention had been accomplished, I would have never existed. I took authority over that curse and cast it from me.

> "Death and life are in the power of the tongue, and they who indulge in it shall eat the fruit of it."
>
> Proverbs 18:21 AMP

My words had voiced that spirit's will.

"Bonnie, put your shoes on. You are liable to catch your death of cold."

"Don't come up behind me like that. You scared me to death."

"I screamed bloody murder."

The expression that was most serious was the one I meant: "I'd rather die and go to heaven than ever have to again live through the agony of these past fourteen years." Until I repented of aligning myself with the destroyer with the words of my mouth, God did not deliver me from the bondage of the spirit of death.

> "This day I call heaven and earth as witnesses against you that I have set before you death and life, blessings and curses. Now choose life, so that you and your children may live...for the Lord is your life and He will give you many years in the land."
>
> Deut. 30:19,20 NIV

Depressing and negative emotions can be expressions of the spirit of death. God does not hover over us with thoughts of death, nor is He the author of death. Jesus came to destroy death's power and to give us abundant life in Him. Jesus desires that we rejoice in the life He has given us and to choose life.

After Frank and Ida prayed for my healing and we stumbled upon the need for deliverance, we all knew I needed more. They began to intercede for me. We were meeting for prayer frequently, but their efforts and my yieldedness did not bring sufficient release. Our home experienced a fracas, and they went into intercessory warfare. Ida Mae awakened in the night; the Holy Spirit gave her a vision of my problem, schizophrenia. This vision was confirmed by Frank's vision the same night of a golden key. He did not understand the significance of that vision; I had not told him about my request for the key.

I was absolutely unprepared for this revelation. My limited knowledge of mental illness told me this was serious, but I had no understanding of the varying degrees. I went into shock.

Schizophrenia to me was craziness, like that in the film "The Three Faces of Eve." It was paranoia, the same word my brother Ed used to describe the man who burned our house. It was diabolical killers in mass murder trials. Was this the key I asked for?

Had Bill contacted the mental health department and summoned them to our home during the following three days, I would have certainly been institutionalized. Paralyzed by shock, I slipped in and out of reality, considered suicide, and today have no remembrance of three-year-old David being present. I have vague recollections of Bill praying for me when he arrived home from work, but those days are virtually blank. The demons knew their time was limited in their house, my body, and they tried to exert their will as best they could while they had the opportunity.

On the fourth day I awoke released of the worst of the torment. I was soon informed that some in the church fellowship were talking about me, discussing if I were crazy, and this aroused furious anger in me. Bill became my defender and protector. Never before had I received such attention and love from him. Later he repented publicly of his previous actions which had contributed to my emotional decline.

Bill prayed fervently for direction, and as a result,

moved us temporarily into our former church congregation to escape the gossip. Our testimony to that pastor, Dale, and his wife Carol, about the power of the Holy Spirit later assisted them in receiving the baptism of the Holy Spirit.

The only information I had been given by Ida Mae was that I was schizophrenic. I did not know then what the components of the pattern were. God spoke to me in a dream and showed me that as I followed His explicit instructions, He would be my Deliverer. He had shown Ida ten fingers. Each one represented a demon. The middle finger on one hand was rebellion; on the other it was rejection. Spirits of insecurity, fantasy, jealousy and even suicide were others.

As I read Psalm 68, the words "dry" and "parched" described my feelings. I was astonished to read that "the rebellious dwell in a dry and parched land." I accepted that the Lord was telling me I was rebellious.

I began to submit to Bill in ways the Spirit directed. Rebellion, rather than being called out and delivered by a minister, was pushed out as I obeyed the inner voice of the Lord. The process took time, over eighteen months. I know with absolute assurance that I have not been under the control of rebellion since that time.

Parting company with the spirit of rejection began one afternoon very shortly after the Lord showed me I was rebellious. I had invited an acquaintance to my home, but was coldly informed that God instructed her not to visit me. I automatically prepared my familiar "pity party," when the Holy Spirit interjected with thoughts of 'spirit of rejection; bind it.' As I obediently responded, pleading the blood of Jesus, the "feel sorry for me weeps" abruptly ceased.

I needed the additional ministry of the body of Christ to completely lose the spirit of rejection. My friend laid her hand on me and prayed for thirty minutes until that spirit no longer tormented me. It tore and wrenched my body as it left, and I wept great tears of release.

When the axe was applied to three root spirits, or strongmen, rejection, rebellion and spirits of schizophrenic personality, we knew we had won the major part of my freedom. When the spirits of schizophrenic personality left, I never again experienced the disharmonious struggle between two persons claiming occupancy in me. I then was called by my middle name, Jean, and "Jean Two" departed from me.

To those who argue that a Christian can't possibly have a demon, I give an answer similar to that of the blind man when he was confronted by the Pharisees, "Once I was blind, and now I see." I say, "Once I was bound, but now I'm free."

When God was finished setting this captive free, I had lost every demon revealed to Ida Mae. I did not lose all of them in one session, but over a two-year period we successfully prayed against each one as they manifested themselves in my life. Each time I was delivered the Lord showed me how to walk in the new freedom, how to adjust to new thoughts and actions and the lack of the old controlling thoughts.

I maintained my freedom with a strategy that the Lord taught me. First I accept the fact that I will experience some rejection and other trials. But I identify with Jesus. Who also faced rejection, for He was despised and rejected, a man of sorrows and acquainted with grief. Therefore I am not overwhelmed. Secondly, I bind the spirit from exerting its power over me in whoever is the tool for the attack and walk away, leaving it all in God's hands.

I thank God *He still sets the captives free.*

PROVERBS CHAPTER 31

(Paraphrased for the modern woman)

by Mary-Etta Hinkle

10. Who can find a truthful woman? For her price is far above diamonds or mink stoles.

11. She never buys extravagantly. Her husband need never resort to embezzlement to pay her bills.

12. She pets him with tender words of loving care as long as there is breath in her body.

13. She is not afraid of sewing projects: new clothes, patches on the old clothes, embroidery, quilts, afgans, crocheting, knitting.

14. She shops for the most economical buys on food. She cans and freezes. She might do gardening.

15. She keeps her spiritual house in order and her physical house also.

16. She is a helpmeet to her husband in every new business venture. She prays in regard to every new decision facing them. She refuses to exhaust herself with unnecessary tasks.

17. She guards her mind and keeps her body strong with proper rest and care.

18. She views her work with pleasure. She stays faithful in the midst of every trial.

19. She might try her hand at the old fashioned art of spinning wool.

20. She is a ministering servant to those who seek her help.

21. She puts her entire family under the blood of Jesus by her faith in Christ.

22. She makes beautiful drapes for her home. She dresses in modest elegance. In her spiritual walk she has put on the King's robes.

23. Her husband is respected in the community.

24.   She makes things to sell. Spiritually she weaves her life in to the righteousness of Christ.

25.   She is strong and stable -- not given to hysterical fears. She is not a pessimist, but looks forward to the future with faith and hope.

26.   She has learned how to bridle her tongue from idle and hurtful gossip and the words she speaks are words of kindness and love.

27.   She manages her household well and will not allow herself to be lazy and sluggardly.

28.   Her children respect her as their mother and her husband is so proud of her that he boasts about her when he shares with friends and acquaintances.

29.   She excels above everyone else in the eyes of her family.

30.   Outward beauty is tricky and deceptive; but the woman who fears and worshipfully trusts the Lord shall be praised.

31.   Her home will bear fruit for the glory of God and her works will be known by many.

Powerful Help on Cassette

Are You Saved? Have You Been BORN AGAIN? Do you even know for sure what is meant by these questions?

If not, we strongly recommend that you send for the tape
HOW TO BE SAVED, or BORN AGAIN!

To receive this informative tape, which can change your life . . . just as it has for thousands of others, when they have heard the message contained on the tapes and responded to it. . . .

Simply send your name and address along with $5.00 to cover all costs to:

IMPACT BOOKS, INC.
137 W. Jefferson
Kirkwood, MO 63122

NOTE: If you honestly cannot afford to pay for the tape, we will send it to you free of charge.

Bestseller II

PIGS IN THE PARLOR $5.95

If you *really believe* JESUS delivered people from evil spirits . . . Then you owe it to yourself to read this book! Learn that it *still happens today!*

This book contains a wealth of practical information for the person **interested in, planning to engage in,** or ac**tively engaged in** the ministry of deliverance.

It is a PRACTICAL HANDBOOK, offering valuable guidance as to determining . . .

> ● HOW DEMONS ENTER ● IF DELIVERANCE IS NEEDED ● HOW DELIVERANCE IS ACCOMPLISHED FOR OTHERS AND SELF ● HOW TO RETAIN DELIVERANCE ● GROUPINGS OF DEMONS (listing those demons that are often found together).

The book also includes a chapter presenting a revelation on the problems of **SCHIZOPHRENIA** which could well revolutionize the way this subject has been traditionally viewed by the medical profession!

THE HEAVENS DECLARE . . .

William D. Banks

More than 250 pages!
More than 50 illustrations!

- Who named the stars and why?
- What were the original names of the stars?
- What is the secret message hidden in the stars?

The surprising, **secret message** contained in the earliest, original names of the stars, is revealed in this new book.

The deciphering of the star names provides a fresh revelation from the heart of **the intelligence** behind creation. Ten years of research includes material from the British Museum dating prior to 2700 B.C.

A clear explanation is given showing that early man had a sophisticated knowledge of One, True God!

$6.95 + $1.00 Shipping/Handling

ALIVE AGAIN!

William D. Banks

The author, healed over twelve years ago, relates his own story. His own testimony presents a miracle or really a series of miracles — as seen through the eyes of a doubting skeptic, who himself becomes the object of the greatest miracle, because he is Alive Again!

The way this family pursues and finds divine healing as well as a great spiritual blessing provides a story that will at once bless you, refresh you, restore your faith or challenge it! You will not be the same after you have read this true account of the healing gospel of Jesus Christ, and how He is working in the world today.

The healing message contained in this book needs to be heard by every cancer patient, every seriously ill person, and by every Christian hungering for the reality of God.

More than a powerful testimony — here is teaching which can introduce you or those whom you love to healing and to a new life in the Spirit!

$4.95 + $1.00 Shipping/Handling

A BLOOD COVENANT
IS THE MOST
SOLEMN, BINDING AGREEMENT POSSIBLE
BETWEEN TWO PARTIES.

Perhaps one of the least understood, and yet most important and relevant factors necessary for an appreciation of the series of covenants and covenant relationships that our God has chosen to employ in His dealings with man, is the concept of the BLOOD COVENANT!

In this volume which has been "sold out," and "unavailable" for generations, lies truth which has blessed and will continue to bless every pastor, teacher, every serious Christian desiring to "go on with God."

Andrew Murray stated it beautifully years ago, when he said that if we were to but grasp the full knowledge of what God desires to do for us and understood the nature of His promises, it would "make the Covenant the very gate of heaven! May the Holy Spirit give us some vision of its glory."

$8.95

BEST SELLERS FROM

IMPACT BOOKS

137 W. Jefferson, Kirkwood, MO 63122

BOOKS _____

___ ALIVE AGAIN	4.95	
___ A LOVE STORY	1.25	
___ DECISION TO DISCIPLESHIP	1.25	
___ GOLD FROM GOLGOTHA	1.50	
___ GREATER WORKS SHALL YE DO	2.95	
___ HOW TO HEAR GOD SPEAK	1.50	
___ IS FAITH REQUIRED FOR YOUR MIRACLE	2.95	
___ KINGDOM LIVING	4.95	
___ MINISTERING TO THE LORD	4.50	
___ MINISTERING TO ABORTION'S AFTERMATH	3.95	

___ MIRACLE BUS TO THE SHRINE	2.95
___ MY PERSONAL PENTECOST	1.25
___ PIGS IN THE PARLOR	5.95
POWER FOR DELIVERANCE SERIES:	
___ SONGS OF DELIVERANCE	5.95
___ DELIVERANCE FROM FAT	5.95
___ DELIVERANCE FOR CHILDREN	5.95
___ THE BLOOD COVENANT	5.95
___ TRIAL BY FIRE	3.50
___ THE HEAVENS DECLARE	6.95

MUSIC & SONG BOOKS _____

___ DELUXE GUITAR PRAISE BOOK	3.95
___ FAVORITE HYMNS ARR. FOR CLASSICAL GUITAR	3.95
___ FAVORITE HYMNS ARR. FOR PIANO	3.95
___ GOSPEL BANJO	3.95
___ GUITAR CHRISTMAS CAROLS	2.95
___ GUITAR HYMNAL	3.95
___ JESUS SONGS!	3.95
___ GOSPEL GUITAR	3.95
___ HYMNS FOR DULCIMER	4.95
___ LITURGICAL GUITARIST	15.00
___ ONE WAY SONGBOOK	3.95
___ SACRED GUITARIST	3.95
___ SACRED ORGANIST	3.95

___ SACRED PIANIST	3.95
___ "SIGNS SHALL FOLLOW" SONG BOOK	3.95
___ SPIRIT FILLED SONGS	3.95
___ CHILDREN'S GUITAR HYMNAL	2.95
___ HYMNS FOR AUTOHARP	4.95
___ HYMNS FOR CLASSICAL GUITAR FOSTER	4.95
___ MORE HYMNS FOR CLASSIC GUITAR-FOSTER	4.95
___ SONGS OF CHRISTMAS FOR AUTOHARP	2.50
___ LITURGICAL GUITARIST (CASS.)	9.95
___ FAMILY HYMN BOOK	6.95
___ HYMNS FOR HARMONICA	5.95

Alive Again!

Bill Banks.
Terminal Cancer.
48 hours to live.
Miraculously
healed!

Name _____	
Address _____	
_____	
For your convenience, you may use either MasterCard or Visa.	
Mastercard No. _____	
Visa No._____	
Expiration Date _____	

PIGS IN THE PARLOR

Do You Know Anyone With
CANCER?
Here's Living Proof GOD HEALS!

500,000 Copies
In Print —

ARE DEMONS REAL?

THREE KINDS OF FAITH FOR HEALING

Many today have been taught that the only way to be healed is to personally have faith for their healing. It is implied, one must somehow 'work up' or develop enough personal *faith-to-be-healed,* and then healing will come. Many have also been told that the reason they remain afflicted is because of their lack of faith.

Such statements in addition to being utterly devoid of compassion, are terribly devastating to the poor hearers. One could never imagine Jesus saying something so heartless. Yet these things are often said today. Even those who have not heard these words spoken aloud have received them through implication from proud, spiritually 'superior' friends who believe that these sick individuals are somehow deficient in faith.

There is good news both for them and for us, because that teaching is wrong. There are more ways of being healed than just the one way, as we have been taught.

In this new book, Bill Banks presents a *revelation* of three main types of faith for healing illustrated in Scripture, and a fourth which is a combination of the other three.

Three Kinds of Faith For Healing   Paper 3.95

FOR ADDITIONAL COPIES WRITE:

137 WEST JEFFERSON
KIRKWOOD, MISSOURI 63122

AVAILABLE AT YOUR LOCAL BOOKSTORE, OR YOU MAY
ORDER DIRECTLY. Toll-Free, order-line only M/C, DISC,
or VISA 1-800-451-2708.